# If You Really Knew Me:

## The Life, The Lessons and The Legacy

Denola M. Burton

Author

Enhanced DNA Publishing

## If You Really Knew Me:

## The Life, The Lessons and the Legacy

Copyright © 2019 Denola M. Burton

All rights reserved.

No portion of this publication may be reproduced, stored in any electronic system, or transmitted in any form or by any means without the written permission from the author. Brief quotations may be used in literary reviews.

Second Edition: Enhanced DNA Publishing
www.EnhancedDNAPublishing.com

Some names and identifying details have been changed to protect the privacy of individuals.

ISBN-13: 978-17336477-0-0

For information and bulk ordering, please contact Denola Burton at DenolaBurton@EnhancedDNA1.com.

# DEDICATION

I'd like to dedicate this book to my husband who has supported me in everything that I have attempted to pursue since we have known each other. Without his love and support, I would not be nearly the person that I am today.

# CONTENTS

| | | |
|---|---|---|
| 1 | Growing Through Life | Pg # 1 |
| 2 | I Didn't Know I Couldn't See | Pg # 4 |
| 3 | A Powerful Weapon | Pg # 8 |
| 4 | "Bee"coming a Champion | Pg # 11 |
| 5 | Invited But, Not Really! | Pg # 14 |
| 6 | A Whole New World | Pg # 18 |
| 7 | It's a Small World After All | Pg # 21 |
| 8 | Thesis or Antithesis? | Pg # 24 |
| 9 | Too Close to Home | Pg # 27 |
| 10 | Baby Maker | Pg # 30 |
| 11 | Another Change | Pg # 33 |
| 12 | Chance Encounter or Serendipity? | Pg # 36 |
| 13 | Harley(s) | Pg # 40 |
| 14 | Passion Realized | Pg # 44 |
| 15 | Instant Love | Pg # 46 |
| 16 | The Lessons | Pg # 53 |

| | | |
|---|---|---|
| 17 | The Legacy | Pg # 63 |
| 18 | Bonus Chapter: Develop Nurture Achieve | Pg # 70 |
| 19 | Bonus Chapter: Becoming a Housewife | Pg # 73 |
| 20 | Bonus Chapter: Significance | Pg # 76 |
| 21 | Bonus Chapter: Why John Maxwell Team? | Pg # 79 |
| 22 | Bonus Chapter: Mirror of Affirmations | Pg # 82 |
| 23 | Bonus Chapter: Becoming an Author | Pg # 84 |
| 24 | Bonus Lesson: Lesson for my Teenage Self | Pg # 87 |
| 25 | Bonus Lesson: Leadership | Pg # 90 |

Denola M. Burton

# INTRODUCTION

Everyone has a story.

On March 14, National Write Your Story Day challenges us to tell our story in written form. However, you may think to yourself, "There's nothing in my life to tell."

It will surprise you once you put pen to paper, or fingers to keyboard and the words start filling the pages. Words have a way of triggering memories. They form a moment in time, and before you know it, there's a story flowing from your fingertips. Even if you never share your story, it can be empowering to know that your life has been filled with richness and you can really get to see who you are and where you've been.

Today, stories are everywhere - they fill blogs, inspire magazine articles, and yes, even novels. More importantly, they are treasures to family and loved ones.

I did it! I wrote my story: "If You Really Knew Me: The Life, The Lessons and The Legacy". That is my story. I wrote my story in 2018 but I felt like I had more.

So on this National "Write Your Story" Day, I am releasing the second edition of my book which includes BONUS CHAPTERS and BONUS LESSONS! Enjoy the stories, enjoy the lessons and create your

*Don't go through life, grow through life.... Eric Butterworth*

# CHAPTER 1

# GROWING THROUGH LIFE

January 1, 2018. The beginning of my "next chapter". This was the first official day of RETIREMENT! After 27 years at Eli Lilly and Company, I was officially retired! When you retire, you have a lot of time to think – reflect. I began to reflect over my life, my accomplishments, my career and my purpose. I realized how very blessed I had been from my childhood, through young adulthood, through to my current status. I have had so many experiences that shaped my life and who I am today. A big portion of those experiences included my career and blessed to be able to retire at 59 years old!

But then I began to ask myself, "What's next? What does this next chapter of life hold for me?" I knew that one big piece of my retirement would be to focus on my family – after all, I still had a 17 year old and a 13 year old with the many challenges that they could present. My reflections made me smile but they also made me realize that I wasn't done yet!

As I looked back over my life, over my career, over everything that I have accomplished and all the things that I have done, I began to realize that I have accomplished A LOT, but more importantly, I have learned so much through so many experiences. As I began to reminisce, there were a lot of things that I could remember and I lot that I had "repressed" – things that I had to either smile because I had forgotten something that was good and it brought back good feelings or things that made me sad because I remembered things that weren't so pleasant. Either way, they formed me into the person that I am and taught me lessons along the way.

Now that I have time to reflect on my past experiences, I feel it is important to capture some of those experiences from my LIFE. This book includes stories that have shaped me into the person that I have become along with some of the lessons that I learned, as a result of those stories and how those stories and lessons resulted in not only my SUCCESS, but also resulted in my SIGNIFICANCE. Significance to me is making a difference – how I gave of myself and impacted those around me. That significance resulted in the LEGACY that I pray will benefit not only those who may read these stories in the future, but those who are reading them today!

Now, don't get me wrong – I'm not sure that I realized that these lessons were occurring at the time that I was going through these experiences. Maybe it was the reflection that helped me appreciate the lessons and the value that they provided in my life.

Each chapter of "If You Really Knew Me: The Life, The Lessons and The Legacy" will give a glimpse of my life, my stories, my history – the good and the bad. Stories that made me who I am and how I became that person. We will uncover lessons that impacted and influenced me and how my life progressed focusing on the following: Patience, Persistence, Common Ground, Excellence, Valuing Diversity and Passion. The legacy that I will leave will be uncovered and from that legacy, you will be encouraged to discover your stories, your legacy, your value by evaluating your life, your lessons and your legacy.

This book has provided that value to me! Retirement isn't the "end" for me – it is clearly the "next chapter" and I'm starting it with sharing and adding value to each of you through this book! As I reflect on these experiences and the lessons, I am able ensure that I am remembering those lessons and applying them in my future endeavors, allowing me to leave a legacy that will live on forever.

I wish the same for you. Enjoy!

*"It's not what I have been through in my life that defines who I am, it's how I got through it that has made me the person I am today."* Unknown

## CHAPTER 2

## I DIDN'T KNOW I COULDN'T SEE

I'm sure that you have heard of "BC" and "AD" – where "BC" stands for the English phrase "Before Christ" and "AD" confusingly comes from the Latin phrase for "Anno Domini (In the Year of our Lord or the Year that Jesus was born). These terms refer to the point in time where our calendar was created and how time is now measured.

Well, I have another way to think of time – "BG" for BEFORE GLASSES, and "AG" for AFTER GLASSES!

I don't remember a lot of my "BG" years – maybe it's

because they were my earlier years and I was so young. But, I think that much of that time was a blur because it was "blurry"! I didn't know that I couldn't see. I walked around in a blur – squinting to see, but I thought that what I was seeing was what I was supposed to see. I didn't know that my brothers and sisters, my cousins and other family members, my friends (and probably even our dog) could see things clearly. I can remember when I was small that everyone would gather around the big console TV in the Living Room – all of us kids were on the floor right in front of the TV. I was always in the front – I thought because I was the youngest, but it was probably because I was getting close enough to see what was on the screen.

It's almost like the saying, "You don't know what you don't know". I didn't know that it was supposed to be different or better. That was clearly my "BG" experience!

Then, I went to school. I didn't go to kindergarten, so my first experience in a school setting was in First Grade. I remember going to school on the first day and I knew I was missing something. But I didn't know what it was. I saw the teacher at the front of the room but I couldn't tell what she was doing. She was holding up big cards but I couldn't see what was on those cards. It looked like blobs to me. Squinting didn't help. I could hear her. I could answer the questions asked, but I couldn't see what she was pointing at. I couldn't see her writing on the board. The teacher finally asked me if I was having problems seeing. That was my first realization that I was having problems seeing. She sent a note home to my parents letting them know that I needed my eyes checked.

I even remember going to the eye doctor. I was excited.

They were going to help me see! The eye doctor examined my eyes. He made me pick which letters and pictures looked clearer, "Better 1, or Better 2", he said, over and over again. He gave me some sample glasses to look through and I could see! Shortly after that visit, I got my new glasses! This was my first day of "AG"- After Glasses!

My life "AG" was awesome! I could see all kinds of things – leaves on trees. Details on people's faces. Colors. Now everything was clear! Would my entire life be different though? Would the vision change open new doors for me? Well, maybe from a vision perspective, it would be better. But not all of my "AG" experiences were enlightening!

I've experienced my share of ups and downs. I can even remember that some of the negatives were the result of my "AG", life-changing tools – my glasses. Those glasses often got me teased. I liked BIG glasses! I liked PINK glasses! Or BLUE glasses! They were THICK glasses! I often got called "Four-Eyed" or "Coke Bottles" or "Blind Bat" or "Bookworm"! And as a result, I became somewhat introverted. It's a good thing that even at a young age, I was strong willed. I didn't let that bother me and I kept to myself and read my books. I LOVED my glasses and I loved the world that they had opened up to me! Come venture into the world of new chapters that began as a result of a "BG" to "AG" experience!

When I think about my "AG" experiences, they took me through the majority of my life but there were some twists and turns. When I was a young adult, I was able to transition from glasses to contact lenses. So for a while, I was "au natural", feeling naked, to not be wearing glasses.

Then I qualified to get laser eye surgery, so a more permanent way to be without glasses. But even that wasn't permanent. As I began to age and my eyes began to age, I had difficulty reading the small print. And then it got more difficult reading the large print. So, I went back to the ophthalmologist and got prescription reading glasses. My "AG" experience had come full circle!

As I think back on that "BG" to "AG" life cycle, I can't help but compare it to other aspects of my life. Just as I didn't know I couldn't see, there are things that I experienced that prior to experiencing it, I didn't even know what I was missing. As I reflect on my life "AG", I think about lessons I've learned as they were made visible and that I was "BLIND" to. Many of those "AG" experiences were "eye-opening" and every one of those "AG" experiences could be viewed as a new beginning. Did those "AG" experiences open doors for me and change my outlook on life to the possibilities ahead?

Well, if you really knew me, you would know. But, if you want to know me, keep reading!

*"Education is the most powerful weapon we can use to change the world"* – *Nelson Mandela*

# CHAPTER 3

# A POWERFUL WEAPON

Education was important in our house – probably the most important thing after religion. There were no excuses and we just had to "get it done" when it came to school. If you got a "C" in any class, it had to be the worst grade and it better not be a "C" o the next report card. There were high expectations for education and no excuse for anything other than excellence in our family! We delivered.

When I was around 8 or 9, our family moved to Virginia. My father was a minister and became the Regional Minister for the Piedmont Tri-State Area (Virginia, West Virginia and North Carolina) for the Christian Church, Disciples of Christ. After two years in Virginia, we moved to North Carolina and stayed there two years, too. I was about 11 or 12 when we moved to Indianapolis, Indiana. Needless to say, we had a lot of transition as it related to school – but even then, we were expected to excel.

I remember my first day of school in Indianapolis at George Julian, School #57 where Mr. Richy was my teacher. I was an introvert. I had big glasses. I was Black. Everyone else in the class was White. I was introduced to the class by Mr. Richy and he asked me to tell the class a little bit about myself. I began to talk and the more that I talked, the more the class laughed. I was devastated and felt like crying! I was wondering why they were laughing at me?

Mr. Rich began to give the class a geography and culture lesson. He explained to the class that I had moved from the Virginia/North Carolina side of the country and that my accent might sound different to them (a blind spot to me because I didn't realize I spoke differently from them). I had a "twang" in my voice and I didn't even realize it. Mr. Rich calmed the class down and then we began our class work. He explained that the class had been working on their spelling words and they were having a quiz. He told me that I didn't have to take the quiz if I didn't want to or I could take it so he could gauge where I was in my education. I decided to take the test.

After the test was over, students swapped papers to grade each other's answers. After Mr. Richy called out all the correct spellings, he asked everyone to raise their hand if the paper they graded had 100% correct. Only one hand went up. The person who graded my test had her hand up. I WAS THE ONLY ONE WHO GOT 100% ON THE TEST! I was the only one who had no idea what words were going to be on the test. I hadn't seen the study guide. I was the only one who didn't know there was going to be a test. I was the only one who excelled!

The whole class cheered!

That experience opened a lot of doors for me. Even for 5$^{th}$ graders, they began to treat me as if I belonged. I'm sure they didn't know, and I know I didn't know, but this was a lesson in diversity. They had been presented with some things that they had never experienced – diversity in the way I looked, diversity in the way I talked, and even diversity in how I spelled!

*"Spelling is ~~difficoult~~ ~~chalenging~~ hard"* – *unknown*

# CHAPTER 4

# "BEE"COMING A CHAMPION

When I was in Middle School (Jr. High School is what we called it, then), I went to school with a boy named CJ Breedenstein. Why do I remember CJ Breedenstein? Because CJ was SMART! Not only was he smart in every class that we shared, every year, he would win the school Spelling Bee. Guess who came in second? Yep, me. I never could get the number one spot and I would be devastated! I remember the word that I misspelled the last year in Jr. High – RECLUSE. Easy word, but I thought they said an even easier word – RECKLESS. So, I lost again!

It wasn't like the current National Spelling Bee. I watched the finals of the 91$^{st}$ Annual National Spelling Bee not too long ago that was held in Washington D.C. The top 10 finalists were between the ages of 12 and 14 years old. I couldn't pronounce most of the words they were given and I surely couldn't spell them. They were given words like HAECCEITAS, PRAXITELEAN, BEWUSSTSEINSLAGE and the winning word was KOINONIA! The finalists would ask, "Are there other pronunciations?", "What is the origin of the word?" or "What is the definition?. They would also ask, "Would you use it in a sentence?" They would be a certain amount of time to ask questions and spell the word. I don't remember doing any of that – they would just give us the word and we would attempt to spell it.

As I watched the 91st Annual Spelling Bee, I wondered if CJ Breedenstein was watching and if he fondly remembered our days in the Spelling Bee???? I remember those years in Jr. High and that every year, after losing to CJ Breedenstein, I didn't give up. I would start studying all over again. I would find new words, spell them, look them up, try to understand their meaning. I'm sure I didn't realize it then, but the devastation that I felt after losing the Spelling Bee created a "fire" in me! That "bad thing" that happened to me (not winning the spelling bee) became a lesson. I learned patience, determination, commitment. As a result, I gained a bigger vocabulary, a better ability to spell.

I know that I learned some valuable lessons. I'm sure the lessons I learned as a result of not winning a Spelling Bee is what gave me the ability to be in Honors classes in High School, to complete High School in the top quarter of my class, to complete my Bachelor of Science degree in Biology, to write a scientific thesis and complete the Master of Science degree in Biology, to have a successful career and make a huge difference to a lot of people's lives in all aspects of my life.

Interestingly enough, this was another lesson that I was blind to at the time, but when I look back on it, the lesson was C. L. E. A. R.!

*"Diversity is being invited to the party. Inclusion is being asked to dance." – Verna Myers*

# CHAPTER 5

# INVITED. BUT, NOT REALLY!

I was excited! It was the first day of High School! As I stated previously, I was a good student and it was expected, in our family, that we excelled in school. I loved school and was excited for this new chapter in my life. I was still introverted, I still wore BIG GLASSES, and I was still Black – so nothing different. I had my schedule for my first year of High School and I was ready to go and conquer my classes.

My very first class of the day was Honors English. I walked into the room, so excited, on Cloud Nine!

But first, let me tell you a little about the school.

Thomas Carr Howe High School – home of the Hornets. Howe was huge – it was on the East side of Indianapolis in an area called Irvington. Irvington was a very predominantly white neighborhood. In the late 1970's and early 1980's, many of the schools in Indianapolis began bussing in order to have more racial balance in the schools. But this was before bussing. We lived within walking distance to the school, in an all-White neighborhood, so it made sense that there wouldn't be many Blacks in our school. I found out later that in my graduating class, there were only 10 Blacks in my class of over 700 students. OK, so back to my first day.

The teacher was meeting everyone at the door to welcome them. She stopped me. Instead of welcoming me, she asked to see my schedule since I must be in the wrong class. I told her, "No, this is the right class – Honors English". She said that this was Honors English but my schedule must be wrong. She asked to see it. I showed her my schedule and that it had Honors English on it. I was confused as to why she thought it was wrong. Even though I was still an introvert, when it came to school, I would get a little more outgoing so I asked her why she thought it was wrong. She told me that she hadn't ever had a Black person in one of her classes! Wow! I was thinking to myself, "So that means that I can't be the first? That means that I must be wrong?" I asked for my schedule back and proceeded to walk to the front of the class to sit down. She looked surprised but continued to welcome other students into the class. Now, here is the ironic part – the teacher was also Black!

We got past that hurdle. I stayed in her class and she accepted me. But isn't it a shame that you get invited to the party (Honors English) but you don't seem to get invited to dance (being given the benefit of the doubt that you are in the right place)? As the year progressed and I excelled in her class, I believe that I opened her eyes to the fact that all students, not just the ones that she was used to having in her class, have the ability to excel and there is no specific color associated with excellence.

I also opened other doors while at Howe. I had an interest in the sciences. I can recall meeting with the school counselor. We had several "programs" to assist students with their future careers. My counselor wanted me to be in the Cooperative Education (Co-Ops) program which in essence was a program designed to help students prepare to be Administrative Assistants. Now, don't get me wrong, I don't have anything against Administrative Assistants, but my career goal at that time was to have a career in the sciences. My mother was a nurse and I wanted to pursue something in the medical field. So, I spoke up! I made sure that the counselor understood that I wanted to be a science major and that instead of Co-Ops, I wanted to major in Biology. Instead, the counselor was able to put me in the "Health Careers" program. Was it race related? Or was it "female" related that he was trying to guide me to an administrative career? Or was it just, being a counselor? We may never know.

In the midst of this experience, I also had some very positive experiences related to diversity. My experiences in the Jr. Reserve Officers Training Corp (Jr ROTC) program. Yes, I joined Jr ROTC! I was accepted for who I was from the very beginning, and yes, I was the only Black person and one of very few females in the program at my High School! I was heavily involved in the program for all

4 years of my High School years. In fact, I led the Girl's Drill Team, earned the rank of Colonel, AND, I was First Runner Up for the Miss Military Ball Queen during my Senior Year!

Another major milestone in High School was that I tried out for and made the Varsity cheerleading squad when I was a Junior. I became the first Black cheerleader that the school ever had.

These experiences may have broken down some barriers, but it also broke down my introvert barriers. I became much more outgoing and my natural personality began to seep through. In my last couple of years at Howe, more Blacks were bussed from other sides of town and the school became much more balanced. I would like to think that I opened some doors for other minority students to be accepted regardless of their skin color or race. You won't see my name in lights at my High School, or in the history journals at the school, but deep down inside, I feel like I made a difference!

*"College is the reward for surviving High School." – Judd Apatow*

## CHAPTER 6

## A WHOLE NEW WORLD

Once I finished High School, I knew that there was no option for me except to go to college! I loved school and since my mother was a nurse, I wanted to do something in the medical or scientific field. I was accepted into Indiana University at Bloomington and began in the summer after graduation. I was a part of a program called "Groups" which allowed Minority Group Members an opportunity to get acclimated to a university life and get a head start on some of the "General" college courses. I LOVED "Groups"! Now, if you remember, I went to a very predominantly white High School. "Groups" was comprised of nothing but Minority Group Members – all African American students. This was my first true experience in an all "Black" educational environment! We were together in all the same classes, socialized together and we were our own little community. Everything went well for "Groups" and I excelled in the classes and the acclimation to college – or so I thought!

After completing the summer "Groups" program, the real world of college began. I worked with the Counselor to declare my major as Biology with a minor in French. I didn't mention that I took French from Jr. High through High School and because of that was able to "Pass Out" of the first full year of college level French. It made sense to make that my minor. After working with the Counselor and reviewing my grades, we set me up with a pretty aggressive schedule for my first year –Zoology, Chemistry, English, French and Algebra. Now, here is what I didn't understand. All my previous school experiences had been on a small scale compared to IU. All my classes (post Groups) were HUGE! Hundreds of people in each class. This was a very different environment – each class was in a huge Lecture Hall where the professors gave "lectures" with very little opportunity to ask questions or get engaged in the class. It didn't take me long to realize that I was falling behind! This was a very new experience for me. I remember meeting with the Zoology and Chemistry professors – those were the classes that I struggled with the most. I got a tutor. I studied. It was way too much! The more I studied, the more they gave me to study. Ugh!

I met with my professors to put a plan in place. At midterm, I was tracking toward a D or F in both classes. OMG! There was no way I could have a D or F in a class and especially not in my Major classes. I knew that the Final Exam was going to make the difference. Both professors told me that if I got a C on the Final, that would be my final grade. I studied. And I studied. I was ready. I took my Finals and I felt like I did ok – not A level work and probably not B level work. But I felt like I had at least made a C. My whole mentality related to school had changed. Prior to college, I would never have accepted a C in a class. Now I was praying for one! Tests were done. I felt good. I met with the professors before leaving school for the semester and both of them told me that I had obtained the C on the Final!

Well, back then, final grades were mailed to the home. I received mine in the mail and when I opened them, I was shocked to the core! D's in both of those classes! What? I met with the professors, how did this happen? I realized that at a school that large, I was just a number – actually my Social Security Number. Everything was computer generated so even though I had assurance from the professor, the final grade was determined by the computer. There was no opportunity to "plead my case" since the school semester was over and all grades were final.

This became a turning point for me. I had a decision to make. Could I get a quality education at a large school like IU? Was it me or was it the school? Or was it a combination of both? After discussing with my parents, I decided to make a change to an environment that would be more conducive to one on one teacher/student interactions. Stay tuned for "It's a Small World After All".

*"One of the wonderful things about going to a small college is you can get into everything"* – Art Linkletter

# CHAPTER 7

# IT'S A SMALL WORLD AFTER ALL

My dad graduated from a small historically black college affiliated with the Christian Church, Disciples of Christ. Jarvis Christian College is a Historically Black College in Hawkins, Texas, a very small town near Tyler, Texas (also a very small town). Our affiliation with the Disciples of Christ Church began with my dad who was ordained as a Minister in this church. Not only did he graduate from Jarvis, one of his brothers graduated from Jarvis and two of my siblings graduated from Jarvis too. As I was going through the struggles at IU, my dad recommended that I try Jarvis. I was against it at first because it was too small, too isolated and too far away from everything I knew in

Indiana. I didn't want to go from one extreme to another but at this point, I knew that I needed to make a change. We began to make plans. I applied, got accepted and started making my way to Texas. The good news was that my sister who had graduated 4 years earlier, was still at Jarvis, not as a student but she lived on campus because she married a staff member at the college. So, I wouldn't be totally alone.

Jarvis was a shocker! It was a beautiful campus located in the middle of "nowhere"! But, I thrived at Jarvis – not only in the classroom, but I got involved. I became a cheerleader, I was in the Concert Choir, I pledged a Sorority! This was my element. I continued my major in Biology. I was able to repeat the Chemistry class and replace the D grade with an A. Since Jarvis didn't have the Zoology class, I couldn't remove that one but my Grade Point Average steadily improved. I became an Honor student. Doors opened for me in ways that I could never imagine.

One of those doors was a program that allowed me to study away from Jarvis for a whole semester. I applied to participate in a program at the Brookhaven National Laboratory in Long Island, NY (Stonybrook). Brookhaven offered this program to students with a major in the sciences at colleges and universities around the country. This program allowed students to spend an entire semester at the Lab doing research with some of the top scientists in their field. In addition, the students would receive specialized class work to aid in their real-world experience of research. It would put students behind a semester in school, but well worth the sacrifice.

I was accepted to Brookhaven, along with two other Jarvis students. An opportunity like this was amazing and I spent the whole semester under the tutelage of Dr. M. A. Bender, leading Cytologist in his field. I was able to conduct my own research project with Dr. Bender and this is where I gained a love for scientific research. I conducted research in Cytogenetics where I studied chromosome abnormalities. The research that I conducted was included in an official publication with me as a co-author with Dr. Bender. I was able to present the findings from the research at two national meetings: Beta Beta Beta Biological Honor Society National Conference and Beta Kappi Chi National Science Foundation Conference. Presenting at these meetings allowed me to meet Dr. John Session, Head of Department of Biology at Texas Southern University. Dr. Session said he was impressed with the research that I conducted and the presentations that I made and he recruited me to attend Texas Southern University to complete a Master of Science Degree in Biology – all expenses paid! I finished my degree at Jarvis in May, 1981 and began my master's degree at TSU in August of the same year.

*"My future is brighter than before. I know life is hard, but with a higher education, all things are possible."* – Zintathu

# CHAPTER 8

# THESIS OR ANTITHESIS?

Three years! It took me three years to complete my Master of Science degree!

I really don't remember a lot of my "life" during those three years! The majority of my time was spent focusing on my education and the research. I didn't really know very many people in Houston (except for those that were at TSU and those in the church that I attended while I was there. So, my main goal was to get my classwork done and work on my research project.

I joined Dr. Session's team at TSU where he was the

Department Head of the Biology Department. I thought this would be an easy program – a couple of years at the most. The classwork wasn't a problem. It was the research. Research results are never promised – never predictable. My research was in the Cytogenetics field again – very aligned with the work that I did at Brookhaven National Laboratories. But very different. The research at Brookhaven was conducted from human blood where we were able to do the chromosome studies by isolating them from cells. My research project at TSU involved animals – in fact mice. Not just mice, but lots of mice. The key to my research was to perform surgery on 1 day old mice and that was quite an endeavor I had to remove the Thymus of 1 day old mice in order to prepare the mice for the actual study. If you haven't ever "thymectomized" a 1 or 2 day old neonatal mouse, you may not understand. But, that was the foundation of my research.

Here is a little biology background: The Thymus is a lymphoid organ in the neck of vertebrates that produces T cells for the immune system (protects the body against infections). The human thymus becomes much smaller at the approach of puberty and an enlarged thymus could be an indicator of abnormality and could lead to cancer. Mice have a thymus that has a similar function to the thymus in humans. It is believed that some cancers in the immune system (such as leukemia) can be treated if a healthy thymus is transplanted into a person with leukemia and can help regenerate healthy immune cells. In order to test this theory, I would remove an undeveloped thymus from neonatal, 1-2 day old baby, mice and then tested them to determine if the mice could remain healthy without a thymus. I also would transplant a healthy thymus into animals with cancer to see if the cancer could be reversed and sometimes we would treat the mice with certain drugs (like chemotherapy) to improve their health. This research was conducted over a 2-year period – many surgeries on 1-2 day old mice and some on adult mice and many procedures and analysis of the data. Obviously, there is a lot more involved and if you are interested, you can read my entire thesis: Reversal of Leukemia Susceptibility in Thymectomized Mice Bearing Syngeneic Thymus Grafts: A Thesis by Denola M. Burton, 1984.

The final step of completing the master's degree was to actually "defend" my thesis. This is a process where I presented the work that I did, defended the research and my results and demonstrated that I had met the requirements of a "Master" of Science in Biology. The review committee would ask me any questions they wanted to in regard to the time I was in school working on the MS degree. My "Defense" day was one of the most stressful days of my life. I knew that I had done the work. I knew that I had completed all the research. I knew that I was ready, but it was now time to prove it. At the end of the 3 hour "Defense", I was asked to leave the room. When they called me back in, they informed me that I had "passed" and had completed all requirements of the Master of Science degree! What a relief and tears of joy were all I could express!

Funny fact: Back when this thesis was "written", I didn't have a computer. This entire thesis was completed on a TYPEWRITER! If changes were needed, the entire thing had to be retyped! Talk about a lesson in determination, patience and persistence, this was definitely an example of such a lesson!

*"If you're offered a seat on a rocket ship, don't ask what seat! Just get on."* – Sheryl Sandberg

# CHAPTER 9

# TOO CLOSE TO HOME

When I completed my Master of Science degree in Biology, I began to look for my first real "job". At that time, I felt like I was familiar enough with Houston that I wanted to stay. Fortunately, I quickly found a role in research at the University of Texas Health Science Center Baylor College of Medicine.

My Master's thesis and accompanying research was in the Cancer field and I was excited that the work that I would be doing for my first "real" job, was in the cancer field. I unfortunately had a connection that made it important that I continue work in the Cancer field.

While I was in graduate school, my mother was diagnosed with Chronic Leukemia. Mama used to tell me that I was going to impact the cancer research world and even save lives due to the work that I was doing! I wasn't sure about that, but I was excited to make a difference and be a part of the ever-changing world of Cancer research.

My area of expertise was in "tissue typing" and ensuring that patients that needed organ transplants or blood transfusions would get matched with the right kinds of organs/blood types. I remember one time when I came home for the Christmas holiday and I was talking to mama about my work and the studies we conducted. She was always fascinated and wanted to hear all about it. She also wanted to know if she could help. After consulting with my supervisor, we felt that we could use her blood to help with our studies. On my last day in Indy for the Christmas holiday, I was able to get several tubes of mama's blood that I took back with me. Upon arrival, I went to the lab and processed the blood and extracted the white blood cells for use in our studies. WERE WE SURPRISED!!!! A normal tube of blood might result in hundreds of cells but due to mama's leukemia and the rapid proliferation of her white blood cells, we literally had THOUSANDS of white blood cells to use in our studies! We were able to identify the specific markers of her blood type and use these cells in MANY of our studies. Mama was so excited to be able to help with our studies and felt like she was making a difference even though she knew that her white blood cells were not healthy for her.

I continued to keep mama informed to the work that I was doing. Our lab had collaborations with the University Hospital Clinical Laboratory and we would perform studies on patients. Some of the work that I did was included in an official publication that was submitted and published in a scientific journal. I wasn't the main author, but I was included due to the work that I conducted. Mama was so proud and I'm glad that she was able to be a part of my research career.

Mama lost her battle with leukemia on December 25, 1996 when she was only 52 years old.

*"It's okay to change. You're not stepping backward, you're moving forward." – Catherine Lo*

# CHAPTER 10

# BABY MAKER

After mama died, I felt like it was important that I move back to Indianapolis. I had a younger brother who was still in high school and I felt like I could really help him (and my dad) during the grieving and transition process. I was able to find a new position before I even left Houston so I moved back home to Indiana.

I began a new career – still in research, but this time I was working at the University Hospital at the Indiana University Purdue University Indianapolis (IUPUI) campus in Indianapolis. I was conducting research in the Reproductive Endocrinology Division where we assisted couples who were infertile. A couple is considered infertile if pregnancy has not resulted after a year of unprotected intercourse. At that time, medical science was only at the beginning of its complex investigation into the process of fertilization. My role was twofold - to conduct male infertility research to improve possibility for couples to conceive and to nurture eggs removed from the female to assist with In Vitro Fertilization (IVF).

While the medical doctors (under the direction of Dr. Peggy Shepard) evaluated the female to determine her ability to conceive, I would do the same thing to determine if the sperm from the husband was healthy and if not, I would conduct research and prepare the sperm to improve their chances of fertilizing an egg. Sometimes the sperm were sluggish and required "a washing treatment" to help them be more mobile. Washing sperm was as simple as collecting a semen sample from the male and rinsing the semen in a sterile environment in order to assess and isolate the sperm cells. Some men had a low sperm count so I would do procedures to concentrate the sperm so they could be directly inseminated into the female or to directly fertilize the egg. Once I performed procedures in the lab, the medical doctor could inseminate the prepared sperm into the waiting spouse. If the female had unhealthy eggs, the medical doctor would prepare the female for "In Vitro Fertilization". For this process, I had two roles: I would prepare the sperm but I would also fertilize the eggs in the lab. This would occur in an adjacent surgery area where I would "scrub in" just like the doctor's and combine the eggs extracted from the mother and the prepared sperm in a test tube and sterile environment. I would nurture them over a 3 day period to help them "fertilize" and develop into embryos. Once they were fertilized, then the medical doctor would prepare the wife for the insemination. This is the really cool part. Once the wife was ready in the surgical area, I would bring my fertilized eggs (embryos) into the surgery room and the doctor would inseminate. I actually was the first person to "hold" their fertilized embryo (or baby)!

So, at the end of the day, I was a "baby maker"!

But it didn't stop there! As you can imagine, couples who go through infertility can be very stressed, anxious and not necessarily understanding of their infertility issues. Because these procedures need to be planned and could require multiple months of testing and implementation, the couples became very familiar with me and the rest of the staff. Since I worked mainly with the husbands to address their infertility issues, the doctors often asked me to come and explain the evaluation of their sperm and the actions I was taking to improve the quality. It seemed like more and more patients asked for me to help with the explanations since they were having trouble understanding the medical explanations from the doctors. I became a "translator" for the doctors and it seemed like the couples became more comfortable with these explanations and the process they were going through. Dr. Shepard approached me and asked me if I enjoyed working directly with the patients. I told her that I absolutely did! She asked me if I would like a promotion – a new role: Coordinator of Reproductive Endocrinology Programs! The main responsibility was to continue the research role in the lab, continue the In Vitro Fertilizations in surgery, but I would also work closely with the patients to better understand their needs and assist them with getting answers to questions they needed to be comfortable in their infertility journey.

I was now in my element – I was able to use my scientific expertise as well as explore the passion that I discovered that I had to be able to help people. This was the beginning of me being able to pursue my passion – at least that was the beginning for finding my passion!

*"One reason people resist change is because they focus on what they have to give up instead of what they have to gain."* - Rick Godwin

# CHAPTER 11

# ANOTHER CHANGE

I loved being a "baby maker" and I loved coordinating the IVF Programs. BUT, and it's a BIG but, I wasn't totally fulfilled. Something was missing and unfortunately, it was financial. I wasn't making much money in this role and as much as my supervisor wanted to financially reward me, I was being paid through a research grant and the pay was "fixed". After much discussion with my supervisor and our department head about options, they recognized that opportunities for advancement were limited since I wasn't a medical doctor and most opportunities we limited to having that expertise. They even encouraged me to seek other opportunities to expand in my career and in addition to being supportive, provided me with additional direction to pursue.

Each year in Indianapolis, one highlight in the city is the Summer Celebration – Indiana Black Expo. The annual celebration serves as a catalyst throughout Indiana to foster relationships between businesses, governmental agencies, educational institutions, youth services agencies, churches and other community-based organizations. One of the major events during the Summer Celebration Black Expo is a Career and Job Fair (now called the Employment Opportunity Fair). I prepared my resume and off I went to the Career Fair. My main interest was to obtain an interview at Eli Lilly and Company! From the time that we arrived in Indianapolis when I was in 5th grade, I can remember people talking about Eli Lilly and what a great company it was. Everyone wanted to work for Lilly! Lilly is a global Fortune 500 pharmaceutical company with headquarters here in Indianapolis and is known for valuing their employees. Lilly has always stood for "Integrity, Excellence, and Respect for People".

So the first place I went to when I entered the Career Fair was the Lilly Booth. I felt that with my educational background and scientific experiences, that I would have a good chance at a scientific role at Lilly. I didn't know what type of jobs they had, but I felt like I was "trainable"! When I got the opportunity to speak to someone at the booth, they asked me additional questions and even though it wasn't an interview, I was able to talk with a supervisor that had a job opening. Now, this is where the "God" moment happened. The supervisor that I was speaking with was the department head at the Greenfield Laboratories and the focus of his research was

FERTILITY RESEARCH!!!! You have got to be kidding me! That was the "Thank you, Jesus" moment that led to me getting my name in the hat! Without feeling cocky or too secure, I was "CLAIMING" this role. So I waited.

Not too long after the Career Fair, I received a call from a representative from Lilly Recruiting and Staffing. The representative told me that I had been selected for an interview!!!! To make a long story short, I was invited to a full day of interviewing with various leaders in the organization and those were the days when people were "wooed" prior to being offered a job. I was taken to dinner and treated like a queen. Socializing outside of the workplace gave me an opportunity to get to see what the culture of the organization would be and it gave the leadership an opportunity to see me in a relaxed setting. Not long after the wooing, I received a call for a job offer! My prayers had been answered! In addition to the SIGNIFICANT pay increase, I would be doing very similar work to what I was doing with the IVF program. I would be supervising male and female fertility studies (in animals though) but this time the studies purpose was to ensure that any medications that Lilly manufactured were safe for men and women of child bearing age to consume. So, for example, if Lilly manufactured medications for diabetics to control their diabetes, we had to ensure that there were no side-affects that would impact either the male or the female if they were to conceive a baby. If we found side effects, we would write the appropriate drug interaction warnings. This was another very noble purpose and I was very excited to begin my new career. The only bad part was leaving the IVF group. They were an awesome team and I knew that I would miss them dearly. It was definitely a sad time to leave but a whole new world was opening for me!

*"What is meant to be will always find its way"* – Unknown

# CHAPTER 12

# CHANCE ENCOUNTER OR SERENDIPITY?

I was excited to go to work! This was my last day working at IU Hospital, IVF Programs, but that wasn't what I was excited about. It had been advertised for several weeks – JEWELRY SALE! What better way to shop than to shop while at work! All kinds of jewelry vendors and stores were going to be on site and during my breaks at work – I could shop! Now that is LIFE!

My friend, Brenda and I went over to the sale – it was our final time to "hang out" together during our work breaks but we were anxious to see what they had at the sale too. Bling over here and bling over there! Both Brenda and I have very outgoing personalities, so while we shopped, we also socialized – with everyone, especially since most of our friends knew that it was my last day to be there. Some of the people we were joking around with the Police Officers and Security Guards that were brought in specifically to guard the jewelry. Some of them I knew since they worked the day shift, but some I didn't know. One "particular" young man caught my eye. My radar went off – he was so handsome! I asked Brenda if she knew him, but she didn't. She did, however, know the other Police Officer that he was standing with. So, I convinced her to go over with me. She introduced us, his name was Phil, and we all had a good time talking. I asked him how come we never saw him on campus and he said that he normally works the night shift and only stayed over to work the day shift to guard the jewelry. This was the only day that he would be working. Pretty ironic that I would get to meet him on my last day of working and his only day working day shift! One of the officers said that he was having a birthday party that night, so he invited all of us to come.

Well, my friend was married so she said she wasn't going to the party. I was really disappointed because I didn't want to go to the party by myself and yet, I felt a connection with Phil and wanted to see if he would be there. I called several friends until I found one that would go to the party with me. So, we went – YAY! We showed up. I really didn't know many people there, so I was specifically looking for the Police Officer/Security Guard group. I found them. Phil was there. As a group, we all just sat around and talked. Phil and I talked some but nothing super special. But I still felt the connection. At the end of the night, I was hoping that Phil would ask me for my number or something – but he didn't. Well, I guess that was the end of what could have been something good.

The next day, I was moving across town. I would start my new job on the following Monday and it was in Greenfield which was about 20 minutes East of Indianapolis and since I lived on the West side of town, I was moving to the far East side. As the moving people were loading my truck, I heard someone come up behind me. It was one of the Security Guards from IU and he was also at the party the night before. He asked me where I was moving and I told him. I told him that I didn't even know he lived in this apartment complex and it was ironic that I hadn't seen him before my last day in the complex. We laughed about it. I then asked him what he knew about the guy, Phil. He said that Phil was "cool people", but kind of shy. I told him that I thought we had a good time the night before, but that Phil didn't make any attempt to get my number or keep in touch. He said that sounds like Phil. I asked him if he just happens to run into Phil, would he give him my number? He said that he would be glad to.

The end? NOPE! On the following Monday evening, I received a call – you guessed it, from Phil. He said that he just happened to run into one of the Security Guards and the Security Guard gave him my number. YES! We talked and that was the beginning of a great relationship. Now, he wouldn't say that was the beginning because he was pretty set in his ways regarding relationships and even told me that he wasn't looking for a relationship – maybe just a friendship. I told him that I was ok with that – I was really looking for companionship – nothing serious. In fact, he stressed that HE WAS NEVER GETTING MARRIED, so he wanted to make sure that I understood that up front. I told him that was fine with me since we were just looking at friendship.

Two years later, we were married!

*"Communication works for those who work at it". – John Powell*

# CHAPTER 13

# HARLEY(S)

My husband, Phil, is a police officer and has been one as long as I have known him. Early in our marriage, he was assigned to the Traffic Unit in his department which meant that he would be on a motorcycle for much of his patrol. He fell in LOVE – with his department provided Harley! That's all he talked about. Harley this, Harley that! His goal was to one day own his own Harley, so he began making plans. He saved. He visited the Harley Davidson shop. He was fascinated with everything about Harleys and just had to have one. Then one day he said he was ready, he wanted to purchase his own Harley. Now, I wasn't a fan. I didn't like motorcycles and I surely didn't want to own one. I also was only secure in him riding the Harley at work because I knew he was trained for it. In fact, he was on the Motorcycle Drill Team, so not only did they ride the Harleys to patrol, they did complicated maneuvers on them. I didn't really understand his fascination with motorcycles but I guess I could get on board. But, there was something I wanted too! My response to Phil was, "If you get a Harley, then why can't I have a puppy?"

Now, you have to understand my husband to know why that was a significant question. First of all, he never had any kind of pet when he was growing up. Second, Phil is borderline OCD and is a cleanliness freak! While we were dating, he often stated, "NO PETS! NOT EVEN A GOLDFISH!". Really? A goldfish, Phil?

So, when I began the Harley/puppy conversation, it was immediately not even up for discussion. I got no response to my question. Life goes on, time passed. Phil looked at motorcycles. He found one. He fell in love. He ordered it. He brought it home. He was in HEAVEN!

Soooooo....... I asked him, "Does this mean that I can get a puppy?" Still no response. But here is something that my husband knew. Happy Wife, Happy Life! One day after an event, my husband took a detour instead of going home. Next thing I knew, we were at the Indianapolis Humane Society. I perked up and said, "We're going to look at puppies?" He didn't even answer, just smiled.

We walked in. Well, if you haven't been to an animal shelter or humane society, you may not realize that there is a strong "ammonia" smell. Phil immediately said, "Is this how you want our house to smell?" I told him that it wouldn't because we would only have one little small puppy, not a building full. He told me to go ahead and look, he would be out in the car.

So I walked around and told the attendant that I was looking for a small puppy that would stay small. That was my only requirement. The sales person showed me around and took me to a kennel with two small puppies in it. He explained that they were some sort of terrier mix – probably a Jack Russell and 57 other breeds, and that one was a boy and one was a girl. The boy was already spoken for. As I reached down into the kennel, one of the puppies came over to me and began to lick my hand and whimper. It's like she was "picking me". It was the girl and she was available. I was in love and she was instantaneously mine! I now understood my husband's fascination with his Harley because now I was fascinated with something! Due to Humane Society procedures, I couldn't take her home with me that day because they had to give shots and spay her. We would need to come back in two days to pick her up.

I excitedly told Phil that I had found my new puppy! I spent the next two days getting ready. We purchased supplies including a crate and got "her room" all set up in our laundry room (as far as Phil was concerned, the room farthest away from our bedroom).

We picked her up and here is what Phil said, "That is the ugliest dog I have ever seen!" I told him that she was beautiful to me. Once we got home we took her to her room and let her explore. But she didn't want to explore the room and her toys, she wanted to explore Phil. She sniffed and she jumped! She loved him! Phil tried to be hardcore but he was very quickly warming up to her. That evening when she was whining because she was in her crate, he went to her room and brought her crate in our bedroom so she would be with us. (Big softie)

So, Phil got his Harley and I got my puppy. And in honor of the inspiration for me having a puppy, I named my puppy "HARLEY"! Now we both had a Harley!

*It's a beautiful thing when a career and passion come together! – Unknown*

# CHAPTER 14

# PASSION REALIZED!

All of the signs were there. Many experiences in my past were indicators that I was a nurturer, a helper, a supporter, counselor and coach. Every role that I have ever had took on a different aspect. Yes, I would excel in my roles, but I found other ways to fulfill my passion. I would take on more. Who would coordinate the Christmas party? Me. Who would be on the Safety Committee? Me. Who would serve on not-for-profit boards? Me. These are just a few of the additional roles that I would take on to fulfill my passion – over and above my regular job.

Until Human Resources (HR)! I was working at the Greenfield Laboratories at Eli Lilly and Company and had just taken a new role – Plant site Safety Representative. I didn't get this role because I was so much of an expert in Safety. I didn't get this role because I knew so much about the plant site and the safety issues. I believe I got this role because of my demonstrated expertise in coordinating, coaching, training, and developing others in my previous roles. This role required all of this. I served in this role for about four years and enjoyed every bit of it. But one of the perks of this role was that my office was right next door to the HR Office and I reported up through the same supervisor as the HR Manager on site. I worked very closely with the HR staff and gained tremendous insight to the roles of the HR professional and the work they did. That is when I began to have career conversations with my supervisor and "sponsors" about potential careers in HR. It was at that time that my HR Representative recommended that I complete some career assessments. So I completed the Myers-Briggs introspective assessment that identifies psychological preferences and how people make decisions; the Insights into Personal Effectiveness working style and relationship style assessment and the StrengthsFinder assessment to identify strengths. Every one of these assessments provided additional support and confirmation that the types of roles that I would excel in were those more focused on coordinating, people development and counselling. As a result of my interest and the confirmation of the tests, I was recommended for my first HR Representative role, supporting the Global Medical organization. This was a perfect fit since I had a scientific background and I was able to understand the Medical business and the work that my customers required HR support for. This was the beginning of the next 20 years of HR related roles.

*"The adoption took time, the love arrived instantly"* – Unknown

# CHAPTER 15

# INSTANT LOVE!

"Something" came over me! I'm not sure what it was but out of the blue, I wanted to be a mother! WHAT? I was 42 years old! What was I thinking? Why not 5 years earlier? Or for that matter, 7 years earlier when Phil and I got married? OMG! What was I thinking?

I couldn't get it out of my mind! I thought about it. I prayed about it. And I listened to God! God opened doors and confirmed that "it" was for me! But, it wasn't all about me and my wants. It was also about my husband, my partner, my teammate, my soulmate. He had to agree.

He had to want to be a father as badly as I wanted to be a mother. I thought that would be a "hard sell" since Phil said from the very beginning of our relationship, that he did not have to be a father. We had that conversation early in our marriage because I was 35 when we got married and I told him that if he wanted children, we needed to have them "right away"!

So, I was scared to have this conversation! We talked about the pros and cons.

Pros: We really enjoyed our nieces and nephews and especially our youngest nephew who spent many weekends with us. We were settled in our careers and were relatively stable financially. We owned our own home and had space to grow. We had so much to give on so many levels – emotionally, spiritually, physically and financially. We were ready to love.

Cons: We were "older" which would mean that there would be a generation between us (all our friends had kids earlier in life and by the time our child was in high school, theirs would be in college or even married). We would need to adopt. I was 42 years old by gosh and there wasn't any way that I would be "birthin" any baby! LOL!

At the end of the day, we weighed the pros with the cons and OUR passion was so strong (once I talked to Phil, he very quickly wanted a family, too) and we began to inquire about the adoption process.

Then the wheels started turning. This was February, 2000. We met with the Children's Bureau to get a better understanding of the adoption process. We attended an all-day adoption preparation class. We had decisions to make. What kind of adoption did we want to pursue? Infant vs older child? Open or closed? Local vs national vs international? We completed a "home study" through the agency which was the process used to determine if we would be successful parents. We were approved and we decided that we wanted a national search and we wanted an infant. Still lot's to do. We reviewed a packet of birth mother's from around the country. We selected several that had a profile that would be acceptable to us (closed adoption where there is no contact after birth, healthy and we specifically requested a girl). After the initial selection of birth mothers, we provided a profile to those birth mothers who then had the opportunity to "pick us back". The final decision was the birth mothers. We had our "first" birth mother match in March (remember, we just started the process in February). This birth mother was in Las Vegas and it looked like everything was perfect. She would deliver in May. So we began the waiting process. We didn't have any contact with the birth mother – all contact was through the agency. We received periodic updates but our job was just to wait! So we waited. And waited. And waited. We finally received a call. The birth mother had the baby and she decided to keep her! DEVASTATION! But wait! I should be happy for her. I should be happy for her family. But I was devastated! I had to tell myself, that God gave me the assurance that this was going to happen and that that child was not for me. I had to tell myself that the child that was meant for us was going to come to us and it would come in God's time. I said over an over to myself: "That child had a mother. I am not interested in a child that has a mother, I am interested in my child. I want to be a mother to a child who needs me. My child will come".

The agency workers were devastated for us. They immediately found one of the other birth mothers who was also interested in our profile. This one was from Atlanta. We were matched again and the baby would be due soon. So we waited again! And waited. Well, that one didn't work either. Her family decided to help her raise her child. It was amazing to us how the birth mother could have such a hopeless situation and yet when the baby was born, they couldn't go through with it. I cannot even imagine what those birth mothers were going through and I cannot even imagine how difficult it must be to carry a child for nine months and turn it over to someone else! So I was torn and on an emotional roller coaster!

So we tried again. Finally, a situation that seemed like there was no way that the birth mother would change her mind. A young lady in a rural town in Texas who was white and the birth father was black. The agency described how she would be disowned once the baby was born and that there was very little risk that this would fall through. So we were encouraged. And we began the wait. By this time, it was summer and the baby was due at the end of July. We were at our family reunion in Missouri when we got the call. She had the baby! We were ecstatic, the agency was ecstatic, our family was ecstatic. We began to make arrangements to go to Texas. In adoption scenarios, there is a requirement that the baby remains in the hospital for 24 hours before being given to the adoptive family so we had to wait until after that 24 hour period before traveling to Texas. Twenty four hours came and went! I was stressed to the max! We finally got the call. The birth mother left the hospital – and took the baby with her! They were just as shocked as we were.

By this time, we were getting discouraged. We had doubts – maybe it wasn't meant to be. Maybe we should just "give up"! No! She was out there! I knew she was!

August 1, 2000, we received a call from the agency. That morning, a birth mother walked into a hospital in Houston and stated that she was in labor and wanted to talk with a social worker about adoption. She had her baby that day. She had a girl. She saw our profile. She wanted us! The agency asked if we were interested. What? Were we interested? That was OUR baby! Of course we were interested! We waited the 24 hour period. We got the call. She was ours! The papers were signed! We could make our flight arrangements!

The next day, we flew to Houston and picked up our daughter right from the adoption agency. It was late at night and as we walked up to the agency door, all we saw was a little bundle with a head full of hair. Our hearts were full and we shed so many tears of joy! We completed paperwork and took her to the hotel.

Over the next week, we remained in Houston where we completed all the appropriate paperwork and bonded with our daughter. We also were able to meet with the birth mother. Meeting with the birth mother was a very emotional experience, where she was able to see the miracle that she created and we were able to assure her that we would give "this gift" the best life possible. Based off that meeting we decided to give the birth mother "a gift". Our gift to the birth mother was to use part of the name that she had given the baby at birth. We had already chosen the name that we wanted the baby to have but we decided to change the middle name so her name became Danielle "Jayvonne". Jayvonne is the name that she had chosen, so we thought it would be fitting to honor her sacrifice by keeping that name as a tribute to the ultimate gift she was giving.

I look back on this experience and realize that God had a plan for all our lives and that we were positioned in the place that we needed to be in to have the child that He wanted us to have.

Four years later, we began the process to adopt for the second time when Danielle was 4 years old. We used the same process for this adoption where we went through the birth mother matching process. This time, we were matched with a birth mother quickly and she requested that we meet in order for her to determine if we were the right family for her child. Since he was only a 45 minute drive away, we actually met with her when she was about 7 months pregnant. She told us her story – how she was 24 years old, already had 4 children, had no job and her boyfriend, who was also the father of her other children, also was unemployed. Neither of them had completed High School or had their GED. She said that she had her tubes tied after her last child so she was shocked when she went to the doctor for what she thought was a flu bug and he informed her that she was very pregnant.

Can you even imagine!

She informed us that she had chosen us to be her baby's family and we met with and spoke with her several more times before she delivered. We worked with the Adoption Agency to finalize all the appropriate paperwork and we invited to the hospital the day after the baby was born. We went to the nursery and were instantly in love! The birth mother signed the papers for the placement to be official and we went to meet with her before she was discharged from the hospital. She had one final visit with the baby and then placed "Ciara" in our arms. Here is what she told us:

"THIS CHILD will never go hungry!

THIS CHILD will never be on welfare!

THIS CHILD will never be homeless!

So I give THIS CHILD to you out of love!"

What a love story! This selfless, unconditional, sacrificial love is the love that I think of daily – every time I look at my girls!

*"No matter who tries to teach you lessons about life, you won't understand until you go through it on your own."* – Unknown

# CHAPTER 16

# THE LESSONS

**Lesson in ……** Patience

*Patience is not the ability to wait but how you act while you are waiting.* Unknown

One strength that will benefit you in every aspect of your life is patience. Patience not only demonstrates an exercise in self-control, that shows that you can handle whatever life throws at you, it also shows high moral standards and that you value yourself and your future.

Tiny, seemingly insignificant seconds from my life – moments in my daily grind, my routine and the interactions that I had, had to be filled with patience. These small moments added up to a bigger sum of experiences that could have been missed if they had been hurried and impatiently orchestrated.

Patience allowed me to suspend judgment long enough to make informed decisions, thus paving the path to a happy and peaceful life. I realize that great things took time.

*Life isn't a race. Take your time and do it right.*

## Lesson in ...... Persistence

*Persistence can change failure into extraordinary achievement – Matt Biondi*

Persistence is another quality that allowed me to accomplish so many positive things in my life. Even though my goals may have been difficult beyond the usual or expected, I was able use patience combined with persistence to persevere and accomplish what may be viewed as impossible. I realized that being persistent took energy and I was willing to use that energy.

In order to demonstrate persistence, I followed these three steps:

- I identified and pursued my passion.
- I determined my "why".
- I held myself accountable.

You can do it too!

*The highly persistent person sees their journey as a series of adjustments that together will take them to their final destinations. They realize that no great achievement is possible without persistence.*

# Lesson in ...... Common Ground

*Sometimes its just a matter of finding a little common ground and then building a relationship on it. Susan Gale*

Miriam-Webster defines common ground as opinions or interests shared by each of two or more parties; opinions or interests shared by each of two or more parts. More often than not, your goals will be compatible, but the strategies you developed to meet these goals are opposing.

I found that especially in my relationships, common ground was not only critical, but imperative to long-term success. I don't think I understood this until I got married. One thing that I recall from my childhood is that I never heard my father and mother argue. I don't know if it was because they didn't argue or if they just didn't let us hear them argue. I promised myself that if I ever got married, I wanted the same for my relationships.

But, it didn't come naturally. I had to learn the true meaning of "common ground" and "mutual purpose" and how to behave so that we had mutual respect for each other. I realized that if there was a misunderstanding between me and my husband (or anyone for that matter), that it was important to understand what our common goals were and how we could get to a mutually beneficial solution.

This took practice. It took a realization that I didn't have to be right just to be right. I had to realize that "our" solution was better than "my" solution.

*With common ground, everybody gets what they want – everybody wins!*

## **Lesson in ......** Excellence

*Excellence is the gradual result of always striving to do better – Pat Riley*

We all know that excellence is demonstrating outstanding results or exceeding ordinary standards. Excellence is when people strive and achieve being the very best they can be.

I always took pride in my accomplishments. Maybe I was guided by a vision or an idea, and then did my very best to make it a reality. I'm not sure my goal was excellence, but the outcome of my hard work was often success.

I also felt that I had to temper excellence with balance. I realized that if I focused on accomplishing my best in too many areas, I would risk neglecting my other values and priorities. I wasn't trying to "be perfect" in everything that I did and I used my strengths and abilities and opportunities to the fullest.

*Whatever our mission is in life, a commitment to excellence brings us closer to living it well and attaining our dreams*

## Lessons in …… Valuing Diversity

*Strength lies is differences, not in similarities –*
*Stephen R. Covey*

I had a lot of lessons in diversity long before the term "diversity" was a part of everyday vocabulary. Miriam-Webster defines diversity as the condition of having or being composed of differing elements: VARIETY; especially the inclusion of different types of people (such as people of different races or cultures) in a group or organization.

Many of my earlier experiences were "race" related when I was too young to even realize it. As I got older, I began to recognize what I will call "discrimination" but due to the values of Patience, Persistence and Excellence that had been instilled in me, I was able to rise above those experiences and strive toward the goals I set for myself. Were there other experiences that I didn't highlight in my "Life" stories? Absolutely. But, they didn't make me who I am today, so I didn't focus on them.

The bottom line regarding valuing diversity is that diversity exists in everything that we do. It is up to us to ensure that in whatever we do, that we are valuing diversity!

Denola M. Burton

***D**ifferent*
***I**ndividuals*
***V**aluing*
***E**ach Other*
***R**egardless of*
***S**kin Color*
***I**ntellect*
***T**alent*
***Y**ears (Age)*

**Lesson in ......** Passion

*Passion is the genesis or genius – Galileo Galilei*

Passion is a powerful emotion! Aristotle said, "Passion is one of the causes for all human action". You can't fake passion. It is the fuel that drives any dream and makes you happy to be alive.

I am a natural nurturer. When I am helping others, I get a feeling of intense joy that makes me want to continue to help others. That emotion is my passion and it keeps me going, keeps me filled with meaning, with excitement and with being fulfilled. Passion created the ambition that materialized into action when my heart was telling me that there are no other options but to pursue it. I know that passion was also the driving force behind not only my success but definitely my happiness.

How do you find your passion? Ask yourself these questions:

- Does something you are interested in doing, drive you to want to go the extra mile to see it accomplished?
- Do you have a "purpose" or "cause" that makes you obsess over it to the point that it's in your subconscious that you have to engage in that "cause"?
- What makes you want to learn more or do more?
- What are you driven to do?

These could be clues to identifying your passion.

*Once you are clear on your passion, you can make your dreams come true.*

*"Your story is the greatest legacy that you will leave to your friends. It's the longest lasting legacy you will leave to your heirs."* – Steve Saint

# CHAPTER 17

# THE LEGACY

In 2012, I had a lot of transition in my life. This was the year that my father was diagnosed with and passed away from lung cancer. Daddy was my hero, my rock, my motivator, my inspiration. He was truly my support system and he was always supportive of my dreams, decisions and choices – whether they were personal or career related. I'd like to think that even though my initial decisions about my education and career were the result of my mother being a nurse, I believe that my passion for helping others was a direct result of the influences from my father. He was a natural nurturer, being a minister, and I truly believe that is the legacy that he passed on to me.

The majority of my career was in Human Resources (HR) which really fed my passion. All of my HR roles focused on being an advocate for the employee – providing HR guidance to employees and supervisors to assist them with tools to be successful in their roles. This spanned a wide array of services from 1:1 consultations to assist with issues or problems in the workplace, to group interventions and workshops to assist with managing performance and developing as leaders. My "customers" ranged from employees who were new in their career to the highest level of management who could even be at the end of their career. Rewarding? YES! Stressful? Double YES! More rewarding than not, though.

There were times when I had to make tough decisions. Take the example of the employee who I had to assist through a situation that resulted in him leaving the company. Tough experience to go through! But fast forward to a couple of years later when I saw that same employee in a social setting and the employee THANKED ME for everything that I did for them. The employee apologized to me for putting me in a situation where I had to go through some very difficult conversations. But, the appreciation was heartfelt because I believe that my empathy and nurturing to the employee demonstrated respect for all involved throughout the process and the employee realized that. Since that time the employee expressed that they had done a whole lot of soul searching and made some very significant changes in their life. Without that situation and my involvement, they did not know whether they would have had those realizations and made decisions that ultimately changed their life for the better.

There were examples like this that I helps me realize the value I provided. I remember other situations where I helped employees through situations that allowed them to course correct and even excel in their careers. There were situations where I helped leaders grow and develop in their role and as a result were able to add more value to the organizations that they were leading. These are the kind of examples that led to a major milestone in my career.

I was contacted by the Vice President (VP) of Human Resources who wanted to meet with me. I had never been called to the VP's office before, so I was quite nervous! After a little "small talk" and checking in, he informed me that I had been nominated for the "HR Impact" Recognition Award! This was an award where the nominees were submitted by HR peers/managers and voted on by a committee of HR leadership. Not only was I nominated, he informed me that out of the many nominations, I had been selected to receive this award! What an accomplishment! This was the "apex" of my career and since the definition of apex is "the top or highest part of something", it fit that definition. I saw this as the highest recognition of my career accomplishment – to be recognized for excellence by my peers!

The notification of this recognition came at a very vulnerable time for me because it was smack dab in the middle of the final months of my dad's life (he had been placed in hospice care in October). I was able to share this recognition with my dad. Daddy passed away on October

30, 2012. The recognition award was given to me in January, 2013. I was told that I would have the opportunity to give an "acceptance" speech since this was such as significant recognition. Unfortunately, due to a change in the format of the recognition event, I was unable to give my speech. But I had really reflected on the value that I provided to the organization and the significance that it brought to those I served and as a result, I had already prepared the speech. Here is what I would have said to my HR community and it truly speaks to the "legacy" of my success and my significance:

*"A legacy. That's what I feel I have, that's what I feel I will leave. My father was my hero and he left me a legacy – long before he passed away. He instilled in me a foundation that all things should be done with integrity, excellence and respect – long before I discovered these at Lilly. He was a nurturer and he passed that on to me –always thinking of someone else first. I have used these characteristics to excel in my role in HR and to make a difference in the lives of those I touch. Just as my dad would say, "We didn't come here to make it, we came here to make a difference and move on". I am proud to have made a difference, not just in my career, but for living a life of significance – making a difference. That is the legacy that I leave to those around me – especially my children."*

*Thank you, to my father for his legacy and to those who have poured into me which allowed me to leave this legacy.*

*Denola M. Burton*

Denola M. Burton

# BONUS CHAPTERS

Please enjoy these bonus chapters that will give you a little more insight into my life since retirement. You will also get some Bonus Lessons.

*Over every mountain there is a path, although it might not be seen from the valley.* Theodore Roethke

## CHAPTER 18

## RETIRED? YES! DONE? NO!

I have often heard of retirement as "graduation". I can imagine that by completing a course of work that spans over 27 years, it could be viewed as a graduation. And if that is the case, it only seems right that once one graduates, they move on to something else.

My something else was my own business. I didn't retire with this business in mind, but the more I thought about what I would do after this graduation, I figured out a way that I could take the best parts of my career and use my experience and expertise to still make a difference in the lives and careers of others.

The main thing was, that even though I knew it wouldn't be easy, I was leaving the most stressful parts of my job back there. This would be a stress free zone! And so I began.

I began to plan.
I began to develop myself.
I began to nurture myself.
I began to achieve.

Thus, the name of my business, Develop Nurture Achieve.

I had to take baby steps though. Here are some of the steps I took to develop, nurture and achieve with Enhanced DNA:

1. I had to develop a purpose. What was my why? I had to figure out what I wanted to do why I wanted to do it and then put together the plan for "how".

2. Preparation and training. I had to ensure that I was skilled up and prepared to serve out this purpose. I knew that I already had a great deal of experience and expertise in my HR career but I knew that I would not have the tools that I had from my corporate job and therefore I would need to develop in new areas.

3. So I got started. The first thing that I did was begin

study toward the John Maxwell Team (JMT) certification process. This would certify me as a Speaker, Trainer, Coach and allow me the use of a huge library of JMT resources on Leadership. It also added to my credibility as an HR professional. I ensured that all of my other certifications were still current: my HR certifications, SHRM – CP and the HRCI – PHR were already current so I was good there. I also became certified as a DISC behavioral consultant.

4. The next step was to put a robust business plan in place. I was able to identify my goals, detail out my objectives, and complete research and development in order to ensure that I had identified the right customer base and was able to serve their needs.

5. I also had to get my business tools in place. I needed business cards, I needed to set up my business as an LLC, I needed a website and lots of things to ensure that I was able to market my business. I couldn't do this alone so I had to invest in others to have a professional set of tools.

Then I began to network. I began to develop my brand on social media. I began to market my business. This has been a great year. A year of learning. A year of developing and nurturing. And even though I am beginning to achieve, the best is yet to come!

*The hardest job I ever tried was being a housewife.*

*Denola Burton*

## CHAPTER 19

## BECOMING A HOUSEWIFE

Once I made the decision to retire, I quickly began thinking about what life would be like without a 9:00 a.m. to 5:00 p.m. job. My youngest daughter very quickly told me that I would fail as a housewife! In fact, she reminded me of that one morning when I overslept and we had to rush in order for her to catch the bus! But, she had a legitimate reason for her theory. You have to understand our family dynamic to totally understand her lack of confidence in my ability to master the art of being a housewife.

Very shortly after Phil and I got married, we both agreed that he would do the laundry. At that time, Phil was a drill sergeant in the army reserves as well as being a police officer, and I believe, he was also a little OCD! He felt like everything had to have a place and everything should be in that place.

The first time that I did the laundry, he politely informed me that he would fold his clothes from now on because he had a certain way that he liked to have them folded. He didn't even attempt to show me how he wanted them folded, but just said that he would just fold them himself. Since I didn't have any preferences on how I wanted my clothes folded, I told him he could just fold all the clothes. I asked if he wanted to wash them too and he said that he would just do all the laundry. Big win for me!

As you can tell, Phil is much more particular about cleanliness and keeping house. At one point I even suggested getting a housekeeper. Now don't get me wrong I'm not a slob. I was just a career woman and he was a career man without much freedom for either of us to spend a lot of time cleaning. I'm just not as particular about cleanliness, well what I mean is that I'm not OCD! Phil actually loves cleanliness and I'm sure he has done the "white glove test" in our home before. So when I suggested a housekeeper he said that he would prefer to keep the house clean himself. So over the past 25 years, Phil has done all the household chores including laundry, dishes, vacuuming, etc. That has been his release (maybe even his stress relief due to his very demanding job). I really believed this was his relaxation and he really seemed to enjoy it.

Now, I love to cook so that is my main responsibility in the home. In addition to keeping "the food on the table", once we had the girls, I became the main source of nurture and support for them. We have gotten very comfortable in our roles - both of us with very demanding careers and yet, both of us very comfortable in our division of labor.

That should give you a glimpse of why my daughter felt that I would fail as a housewife. Well actually, I informed her that if they were expecting me to instantaneously become a housewife, then I might just not retire! That was not the plan for my future. I am so glad to know that even though I have picked up some of the household responsibilities, Phil never expected me to become a housewife and he still continues to keep the house clean.

As I said, it's his stress reliever.

*One is too small of a number to achieve greatness.*
*John C. Maxwell*

# CHAPTER 20

# SIGNIFICANCE

My word for 2019 - Significance!

Where are you in your life and career? Are you just surviving? Or are you somewhere between "Success" and "Significance"? Success is the result of the things you have accomplished - your education, your career, even things you obtained for personal gain. But to reach significance, you have to realize that success is not enough. When you live a life of significance, you are making a difference for others. Significance means you have learned to give to others, you have learned how to share with others and you live beyond yourself to help others.

I can recall so many times when I felt like I was a success.

In my education. I was very pleased at the level of education that I achieved. Not everyone can say that they have both a bachelor's and master's degree I science! They years that I "struggled" through school were well worth the effort. I can remember when I finally finished my master's degree, that I only weighed 105 pounds! That is teeny compared to the hefty frame that I carried as a cheerleader in high school – probably right around 130. I missed many a meal and worried my way down to that small of a frame. However, don't fret for me, I gained it all (and much more) back over the years!

In my marriage. Over twenty-five years! Anyone can have a wedding but it definitely takes three to have a marriage. Oh, I haven't mentioned the third? It takes GOD being at the head of the house to guide our steps and keep us grounded with each other. Oh, it helps being "evenly yoked" and knowing how to communicate, but without God, we would not have made it. Whenever we had any kind of disagreement or issue, we would take it to God! And through it all, God has blessed us and sustained us!

In motherhood. As I shared before, I didn't "birth" any children but I have been a mother none the less! Once my children were placed in my arms, they were instantly mine and instantly loved! This is a role that I will always treasure – seeing your own growing up to be just like you and excelling. I will continue to pray over my children to be the best that they can be.

In my career. Yes. I am very proud of all my career related accomplishments. You read about them – from scientific research to finishing my "formal" career as an HR professional. Note: My entrepreneurial career is not over yet! I didn't stop there. I am in my glory years because now I feel like in addition to having a successful career, I can move even further into "significance".

As I look back over my life, I can see where I have had significance but now is the time to really let that significance shine through. Everything that I do, I am constantly asking myself, how can I make a difference and does this contribute to my life of significance.

So, live a life of significance – be unselfish, add value, make a difference!

*Success is: Knowing your purpose in life, growing to reach your maximum potential and sowing seeds that benefit others. John C. Maxwell*

# CHAPTER 21

# WHY THE JOHN MAXWELL TEAM?

**What does it mean to be a John Maxwell Certified Team Member?**

Last year I completed my John Maxwell Team (JMT) Certification in Orlando, Florida. I have often been asked what it means to be John Maxwell Certified so I thought I would share my experience.

After 20+ years of conducting HR specific training and workshops and speaking as an HR Professional in the corporate world, I was now going to have the opportunity to focus on speaking, training and coaching in my own business and utilize the tools associated with the JMT. So after completing countless hours of study and listening to certification teaching calls, I completed the certification process. Now what would I do with it?

## What is the benefit of John Maxwell Certification?

The JMT is a group of certified coaches, trainers, speakers and professionals who have been equipped with leadership training based off the 45+ years of influence and leadership know-how from the heart of John Maxwell that is only available to this elite group of certified JMT members. Through the proven Maxwell method, John provides key leadership, entrepreneurship, speaking, coaching, selling and mindset principles that come to life. As a member of the John Maxwell Team, we are able to use the bank of resources based off the many books authored by John Maxwell in addition to the John Maxwell staff who provides ongoing support and growth through a proven leadership curriculum.

## How does Enhanced DNA: Develop Nurture Achieve use these resources?

Enhanced DNA: Develop Nurture Achieve is equipped with the very best leadership skills, tools and resources to make our clients more successful in life and in business. From the pool of over 100 books that John

Maxwell has written about leadership and personal develop, we are poised to coach, teach and speak on John Maxwell programs and books. These can be stand alone or incorporated into existing Enhanced DNA workshops.

## What does John Maxwell Certification mean for our clients?

The JMT philosophy is built upon the principle of adding value to others every day and focusing on personal growth. That is what we do – whether it is through one of the many John Maxwell curriculum or programs or whether it is through one of our customized programs developed especially for the client. Our goal is to focus on our own personal growth, equipping ourselves with the tools needed to equip others to be the best that they can be. We believe that people deserve to be successful and that everyone has untapped potential. We can help bring out that untapped potential.

Are you ready to grow?

*I believe in the power of positive thinking*

# CHAPTER 22

# MIRROR OF AFFIRMATIONS

Are you ready to have a breakthrough? Try this mirror exercise to make a difference in your life and the lives of others around you.

I recently attended a virtual series of workshops by Lisa Nichols "Power Jam 2019". They were absolutely AMAZING! On Day 2, Lisa shared an exercise of empowerment and affirmation and I wanted to share it with you.

Before we can make a difference in others' lives, we first have to make a difference in our own life! This exercise can be the first step to making that difference.

So here it is:

Stand in front of a mirror and look at yourself as if you were looking at your best friend with love, compassion and no judgement. Complete the following sentences:

1. Say your name first -- "Denola, I'm proud that you …" (list 7 different things you are proud of or can celebrate. If you are over 35, they should be things from ten years ago or more.)

2. Say your name first – "Denola, I forgive you for …." (7 different things consciously cutting the shackles to blame, shame, guilt and anger.)

3. Say your name first – "Denola, I commit to you that …." (7 different things you are going to do.)

If you do this exercise (and really are honest with yourself), you will make a breakthrough in your life and will be able to impact others and demonstrate significance to others. It's just like the song from the late, great Michael Jackson, Man in the Mirror, it all starts with you!

### Man in the Mirror
### Michael Jackson

I'm starting with the man in the mirror
I'm asking him to change his ways
And no message could have been any clearer
If you want to make the world a better place
Take a look at yourself, and then make a change

*Sit down to write what you have thought, and not to think about what you shall write.*

*William Cobbett*

## CHAPTER 23

## BECOMING AN AUTHOR

I didn't set out to be an author. I guess you would say that being an author found me. How? Let me tell you....

As I developed my business and began to not only prepare workshops for my clients, I also actually began to deliver workshops for my clients. I am a true believer in the power of "stories" as a way to not only teach a lesson but to reinforce a lesson. So, as I conducted my workshops, I would tell stories. Stories from my life. Stories that taught me lessons. Stories that reinforced the concepts that I was teaching.

I'm sure that my girls would roll over if they realized

how many stories had been shared about them in my workshops! But stories make the speaker more believable, more credible, more human. Participants feel like they can relate to your stories and begin to compare them to situations that they have had where they then can learn the lesson that is being taught.

The more that I told stories in my workshops, the more that I realized that I needed to write those stories down (my memory isn't what it used to be!). As I wrote the stories down, I began to realize that not only were the stories relevant and could teach a lesson, they were my autobiography of sorts! THAT is when I realized that these stories could become a book.

Would it be a best seller? Maybe not. Would it be sold world-wide? Maybe not. My goal was not for fame or fortune, but to share the stories, help someone else learn a lesson and hopefully make a difference in someone's life.

Interestingly enough, the "author" bug bit me and now I am hooked. I want to learn everything there is to know about writing about being an author and even about publishing. I want to make a difference in other prospective author's lives. I have come across so many people who have told me that they either wrote a book, are writing a book or want to write a book but they don't know where to start. I want help them. They have value inside of them that needs to be shared with others.

So, on to the next chapter – stay tuned for more books from me and more books published by me and my company, Enhanced DNA Develop Nurture Achieve.

*No regrets in life, just lessons. Unknown*

# BONUS LESSON

**Lesson** …… for my Teenage Self

Last year I was able to do a keynote speech for an organization here in Indianapolis, The Center for Leadership Development, that works with youth. One of their programs is called "Precious Miss". This program is an all-girl program designed to guide young ladies between the ages 11 and 14 (grades 6-8), through a process of self-awareness and enlightenment. By participating in various interactive modules, The Precious Miss program is aimed to help these young "Misses" increase their self-esteem, develop a better understanding of self-worth and to explore character traits which may heighten or hinder the pursuit of excellence.

The keynote speech that I delivered was actually focused on myself. I wanted to share with these young students (and their parents), that I didn't do everything right as a teenager and that I had some lessons that I would share with my teenage self.

My first lesson that I would tell my teenage self:

*"Good times become memories and bad times become lessons."*

It is important to realize that everything happens for a reason. We don't get to choose what happens in our life, but we do get to choose our response to what happens.

Life is filled with good and bad. Some of the good and some of the bad will find me. I don't determine the good and I can't always escape the bad. What I can do is to always have a positive attitude that the good will get better and the bad won't be so bad.

My second lesson to my teenage self:

*"Today Matters"*

Today is the only day you have. Yesterday ended yesterday. Don't dwell in the past and ponder on past mistakes. Learn from yesterday so that you can impact tomorrow. Each day we are given 86,400 seconds and we choose how we are going to use them. What we have to realize is that if we don't use them, we will lose them. There is no way to get them back. What we don't accomplish today will always be lost.

I stressed that as a Precious Miss, they completed six weeks of self-discovery and positivity and that each one of those "yesterdays" will impact their "tomorrows". The question they needed to ask themselves was:

> What am I going to do TODAY as a result of what I learned yesterday?

Today is the day to begin using what you learned yesterday. Even if you only take one thing that you learned as a Precious Miss and use it for good, you can do that Today!

I think back to my teenage years and wonder if I had given myself these positive words of affirmation, would I have made better use of my TODAY's?

My third lesson I would tell my teenage self:

> *"We didn't come here to make it, we came here to make a difference and move on"*

This is the quote that my father instilled in me after I became an older adult. I wish I had focused on this in my earlier years – even as a teenager. I'm sure I would have taken advantage of a lot of opportunities that I probably missed because I didn't have that mindset. The one thing I stressed to these Precious Misses is that they have the opportunity to make a difference and they can do that now. They can make a difference as a student. They can make a difference with their friends. They can make a difference with their family. And they can do it TODAY!

# BONUS LESSON

**Lesson in** ……. Leadership

Whatever your role in life, you can improve your impact on others and your relationships by becoming a person of Influence – in other words "a leader". I recently spoke to a group of High School students where we discussed leadership and when we boiled down the definitions of leadership, we all agreed that it could be summed up with this one word – Influence.

So what is influence and why do we need it? Here are 5 things to consider when determining your level of influence – as a leader!

People of influence add value – to themselves and to others.

Increasing your leadership is increasing your influence (and vice versa)

- As a leader, you attract who you are, not who you want. Think about it and ask yourself, "What are the characteristics of people that you want to lead or influence?" In order to attract those people, you have to exhibit those characteristics.
- Our value as a leader and our influence level increases when we influence at a time when people need it the most. Leaders sense teachable moments. They sense breakthrough places. They sense when change is possible. And then they take action.
- Determine your motives for wanting to lead. If your motives are sincere you can successfully lead because effective leadership is first based on trust.

Everyone influences someone. The question is whether the influence is for the good or for bad. Our goal should be to equip and develop others – that, my friend, is leadership and influence!

*Life is a long journey, with problems to solve, lessons to learn, but most of all, with experiences to enjoy. Let's enjoy!*

# ABOUT THE AUTHOR

Denola M. Burton is the Founder and CEO of Enhanced DNA: Develop.Nurture.Achieve, LLC. Denola is a natural nurturer and brings her 20+ years of Human Resources experience and expertise to challenge everyone to grow and develop wherever they are in their life or careers.

Denola holds a Bachelor and Master of Science degrees in Biology. After beginning her career in the sciences, she transitioned into HR in 1996 where she began to live her passion! Denola is certified as a Professional in Human Resources from both the Society for Human Resource Management (SHRM-CP), and the Human Resource Certification Institute (HRCI-PHR). She is a Certified DISC Behavioral Coach through Institute Success and is a Certified Speaker, Trainer, Coach with the John Maxwell Team.

Through Enhanced DNA: Develop Nurture.Achieve, Denola is poised and equipped to **develop** and **nurture** individuals and organizations to **achieve** and "Enhance Your Leadership DNA", "Enhance Your Communication DNA", and "Enhance Your Performance DNA". Denola's goal is to help everyone she encounters to recognize success, but also how they can live a life of significance. She does this by motivating individuals to identify and embrace their strengths in order to stretch to make a difference in all they do.

Denola retired in December, 2017 from Eli Lilly and Company, a Fortune 500 pharmaceutical company where her career spanned over 27 years. She has been married to her husband, Phillip, for over 25 years and they have two daughters, Danielle and Ciara. In addition to becoming an author, she now divides her time with her business, being an author and her family.

Connect with me:

Email – DenolaBurton@EnhancedDNA1.com

Website – www.DevelopNurtureAchieve.com

Facebook – Enhanced DNA

Instagram – @Enhanced_DNA

Twitter – @EnhancedDNA

## Enhanced DNA: Develop Nurture Achieve, LLC

Denola M. Burton, CEO and Founder

## Workshop Options:

- Emotional Intelligence: How Do I Get It?

- Communicating With Others – It's About Connecting

- Navigating Your Career

- Managing Through Differences (Diversity)

- Discover Your Strengths

- Coaching for Success

- John Maxwell's - Leadership Game (a fun and comprehensive way to learn how to improve leadership within an organization)

- So You Want to Lead? Then Do it!

- How to be a REAL Success

- Bringing Behaviors and Performance to Life Through DISC

- How To Have A Successful Book Launch

- Supervisory 101: How to Be an Effective Leader

# If You Really Knew Me: The Life, The Lessons and The Legacy

Denola shares inspiring experiences from her life, the lessons she learned from those experiences and the legacy that she leaves for her friends and especially her family. "If You Really Knew Me: The Life, The Lessons and The Legacy" provides a touching, funny, inspirational, in-depth overview of various chapters of Denola's life. The goal of this reflection is to encourage you to look at your own stories and experiences that have made you the person that you are. Once you begin to reflect on those experiences, you will see that you have also learned lessons along the way and that those lessons have helped you establish your own legacies that can impact others long after you are gone.

Enjoy the stories, enjoy the lessons and begin to develop your own legacy!

If You Really Knew Me: The Life, The Lessons and The Legacy

Enhanced DNA: Develop Nurture Achieve
Publishing Division

Denola M. Burton

www.ingramcontent.com/pod-product-compliance
Lightning Source LLC
Chambersburg PA
CBHW031408040426
42444CB00005B/466